EXTRAORDINARY
HOPE

EXTRAORDINARY
HOPE

AL MOZINGO

Extraordinary Hope
Copyright © 2019 by AL Mozingo. All rights reserved.

No part of this publication may be reproduced, stored in a retrieval system or transmitted in any way by any means, electronic, mechanical, photocopy, recording or otherwise without the prior permission of the author except as provided by USA copyright law.

The opinions expressed by the author are not necessarily those of URLink Print and Media.

1603 Capitol Ave., Suite 310 Cheyenne, Wyoming USA 82001
1-888-980-6523 | admin@urlinkpublishing.com

URLink Print and Media is committed to excellence in the publishing industry.

Book design copyright © 2019 by URLink Print and Media. All rights reserved.

Published in the United States of America

ISBN 978-1-64367-878-8 (Paperback)
ISBN 978-1-64367-877-1 (Digital)

27.09.19

EXTRAORDINARY HOPE

This book has taken years to write. It is the third of a trilogy of the Theological aspect's faith, hope, and love. I am now making it available to all who wish to develop, increase, and internalize extraordinary hope in their lives more fully. The book will take one from beginning hope, hope in God, hope that grows, and hope to eternal life. This hope within one can move into other stages, as it grows, it will move into mature hope, and hope that is truly one that is transformative.

After writing about love and faith; I now embark upon hope. It is actually a continuation on the theme of "Getting to Agape" to move one toward God's unconditional love, the perfect love of God. The three theological virtues of faith, hope, and love are given to us from God! I now round out with this third book the trilogy, the original trilogy, faith, hope, and love. We all need to learn as much as we can about the things of God. As one reads through the book there will be an increase of God's influence in your life. The book provides insight, meditations, inspirations, affirmations, devotions, and even some poetry. This book will help one gain understanding how to live out one's life of hope more fully. It will help open the spiritual realm of God's grace into your life.

This book draws one into a journey toward knowing God and assisting one to incorporate God into one's life. We are each on a journey to God. We need to transform our very life, our self, into a life of love.

Al Mozingo

> May the fire in my heart burn intensely,
> May the light in my heart shine brightly,
> May the love in my heart love eternally.
> —Al Mozingo

Contents

Extraordinary Hope 5

Chapter 1: Introduction To The Journey 9

Chapter 2: Hope That Grows 21

Chapter 3: Hope That Matures 38

Chapter 4: Hope That Transforms 47

Chapter 5: The Journey Continues 53

Chapter 6: The Final Steps 64

Chapter 1

INTRODUCTION TO THE JOURNEY

As I start this first chapter it is considering our own experience of God. We all have an innate desire to know and love God. This changes as we become older and more mature. We have this longing within us to journey toward our creator. God is calling us. Do we hear the call within, a desire to unite with our creator? We all listen in the quietness of our heart for that call.

QUIETNESS

Heavenly Father, God Almighty
I look for you in quietness

Jesus Christ, Our Salvation
I look for you in quietness

Holy Spirit, Spirit of Truth
I look for you in quietness

> Heavenly Father, Holy One
> I listen for your love
>
> Jesus Christ, Messiah
> I listen for your grace
>
> Holy Spirit, Spirit of Light
> I listen for fellowship

HOPE IN WHAT?

As I meditate on a book about hope many things come to mind. Probably the most common idea is the possibility living with Almighty God – the father, son, and Holy Spirit – forever and ever.

One day when I was reading a devotional book of mine entitled *My Imitation of Christ*. While reading I came across a passage about hope. Within the pages are many ideas about consolation and admonitions. In this particular chapter, there is a focus on peace, there's a sentence about hope. I am quoting it below:

"This is my hope and my only comfort: to fly to Thee in all tribulations, to confide in Thee, to call on Thee from my heart, and patiently to look for Thy consolations."

Note: I received this little book from a retreat I attended at a Monastery in Southern California. It is a small book, but almost 500 pages! I have been reading it on and off for a little more than four years. [1]

THE LIGHT OF HOPE

Each one of us lives in darkness to some degree. It is because we have a fallen nature. We all have sinned. We all have fallen short. We have the same inclination, the same tendency, as Adam and Eve; to sin!

Jesus came into the world to tell us what his pure and holy light is all about. We find in repentance to him and the way to the light. God will forgive us. But what is the prerequisite to forgiveness? It is we must take the step of true repentance, with a contrite heart.

To overcome the darkness and to bring in the pure and holy light of Christ is truly our hope. We all hope to be reconciled to God through forgiveness. Therefore, we have an attitude God wants us to have. That attitude is one of forgiving one another of their transgressions against you. Then let your light show!

In hope we believe if we do for the least of our brothers and sisters we do for Christ. Therefore, we show mercy and let our light shine. Sometimes we help, encourage, and love others; we pass on the light of Christ's love and forgiveness on to others. This in itself is where we give people hope for God's holy light to come into their life and change things.

This is what the light does! It will change things with the hope of life eternally with the Father, Son, and Holy Spirit. We find that the darkness within begins to fad. We find that the darkness gives way to the light and hope. We find the Fruits of the Spirit (love, joy, peace, patience, kindness, generosity, faithfulness, gentleness, and self-control), start to light up our world and the world around us.

With the knowledge and understanding, this light and hope starts to brighten our life. We are enlightened to a point of wisdom. Others begin to benefit from our life and start to gain awareness and knowledge of the holy light to all the world, Jesus Christ the holy light.

To receive Jesus and his glorious light is to receive the second Adam as your personal Lord and Savior. Jesus is our perfect model so that we can change. The Holy Spirit leading us and guiding us; let your light shine forth!

HOPE IS …

What is hope anyway? The dictionary may say something like: an anticipated desire or a belief in fulfillment of that desire. There is much more than that when we think about hope as it refers to the Christian. We know the end of hope is eternal life with God forever and ever. What else is there? There's much more!

> Hope is an optimistic viewport
> Hope is a gift from God
> Hope is joy in our hearts
> Hope is happiness reigning inside
> Hope is a deepening of faith within
> Hope is seeing things differently
> Hope is knowing that God loves us
> Hope is our yielding to the Holy Spirit
> Hope is love within our very souls
> Hope is wanting to be like Christ
> Hope is our desire to be with God
> Hope is our love shown in action
> Hope is eternal life with God forever

As we read through what hope is we find ourselves changing. We are renewed each time we gain more knowledge and understanding. We will advance our spiritual life to a deepening relationship with the Trinity. The way we think and do things will change. Our words, thoughts, and deeds have gone through a transformation. Our love, faith, and hope have changed. We are new!

CRYING OUT TO GOD

Each of us in our brief lives on the earth will come into trials and tribulations from time to time. We all come to a point where in desperation we cry out to God. We ask with our heart for God to help us. In the scriptures, Psalms 145:14, it indicates that the Lord supports all who are falling. Are you falling? It also states that God rises up all who are bowed down. Do you humble yourself to the Lord God Almighty? We need to keep a humble attitude and have an attitude of gratitude. We need to sincerely humble ourselves to God.

In Psalms 34 it states, "When the just cry out, the Lord hears and rescues them from all distress ... and the Lord redeems loyal servants." So, are you a loyal servant? Does this scripture want you to become a loyal servant? So, we need help from the Holy Spirit to become humble and just. This is very difficult to do. We need to strive for a deep spirituality that will help us to live God's will.

A PRAYER FOR DIVINE FAVOR

O'Lord, restore good fortune

O'Lord, forgive us, your people

O'Lord, pardon all of our sins

O'Lord, abandon your anger

O'Lord, give us life to its' fullest

O'Lord, we will listen to the word

O'Lord, grant us your salvation

O'Lord, give us prosperity

O'Lord, show us your love

HOPE IN BEING CHOSEN

As we read the Bible we find stories of many that are chosen by God for specific tasks. We read in the Old Testament the works of Abraham, Noah, and Moses. In the New Testament we see stories about Peter, Paul, and Jesus. What about our story?

Have we been blessed by God with seeds of greatness? Has God given us through his grace, skills, and abilities to rise to the challenge? What challenge is that? The challenge of using the gifts and talents for building up God's Kingdom! We need the willingness to accept God's gifts and then use them with perseverance.

Most of us want to make a difference with our life. We all have within us a certain about of potential; or what we can accomplish and who we can be. Do we want to be one of the holy ones chosen? In general, the sky is the limit. As a child of God, you are infused by supernatural powers from above. You hope to become an apostle of Christ and to be Christ like. You want to love and serve the Lord. Seize the opportunity!

You are transformed to holiness if you wish it. You just need the desire to become holy and work at it. I always tell people they are only as closed to God as they chose to be. God will help, ask for his help. Awareness of your sinfulness is one of the first steps. Be humble; ask for his forgiveness, he will forgive sin within your life. You can be transformed with the Holy Spirit leading and guiding you.

Each person born has the propensity for greatness in his or her life. Remember greatness in the eyes of the world, might be different that greatness in God's eyes. Do you want to be an apostle of Christ? Let's review some of the items that were discussed above:

- ✓ Ask for forgiveness
- ✓ Destined for greatness

- ✓ A desire to make a difference
- ✓ Potential is realized
- ✓ One of God's apostle's
- ✓ Infused with supernatural power
- ✓ Transformed into holiness
- ✓ One of the Holy One's
- ✓ A child of God

Okay, you are destined for greatness. You want to make a difference. What does that look like? In other words, how has it manifested in your life?

Holiness Manifested in Your Life

- ✓ You have surrendered your heart to God
- ✓ You exhibit a humble attitude
- ✓ You turn from sin and repent
- ✓ You exhibit a selfless spirit
- ✓ You help and encourage others
- ✓ You love God and one another
- ✓ You serve God and one another

HOPE IN THE I AM

When Moses asked God, "The Burning Bush" his name – it was said that God responded with "I Am." In the eighth chapter of John, when Jesus was conversing with the Jess, he told them "I AM" and "Many came to believe in him." Jesus also said, "I am the light of the world. Whoever follows me will not walk in darkness, but will have the light of life." (John 8:12) This I AM is an expression from Jewish tradition that was understood as Yahweh or God. Jesus is indeed the Son of God, the second person of the Holy Trinity. The below information was inspired from a meditation following a reading from John 8:

> I am your shepherd
> I am here to provide for you
> I am rest for the tired
> I am goodness
> I am your strength
> I am forgiveness

Jesus can forgive us from our sins and deliver us from hopelessness. Jesus can heal us and give us rest. There's more:

> I am love
> I am with you
> I am your righteousness
> I am almighty God
> I am the most high
> I am the Lord of all
> I am the creator of the universe

Jesus is the word. Jesus is the way, the truth, the life. Jesus is our redeemer that brings us reconciliation to God the Father. Jesus is the Savior of the world. Jesus brings everlasting life, joy, and peace to all who believe in him.

HOPE IN THE GOODNESS OF GOD

Each morning I usually pray and then do some reading; I read the Bible and a daily devotional guide with a meditation. I sometimes read a spiritual book of some type to inspire me and to broaden my insight. The following information has been obtained from some of these daily readings:

- ✓ You are created in God's image and likeness.

- ✓ You have an internal drive to be self-giving.
- ✓ Your job is to help build up the body of Christ.
- ✓ You know only Jesus can draw us into union with God.
- ✓ You should never stop pursuing Jesus.
- ✓ You will never stop becoming more like Christ.
- ✓ Your quest is to be one with the Lord.
- ✓ You repent and all of heaven rejoices.
- ✓ You are seeking out Christ.
- ✓ You can move beyond your imperfections.
- ✓ You are to help build up the Kingdom of God.
- ✓ You should confess that "Jesus is Lord."
- ✓ You know that God has great Love for you.
- ✓ You know God has a plan to you!
- ✓ You embrace salvation from Jesus Christ our Savior.
- ✓ You are a citizen of God's Kingdom, help build the Kingdom.
- ✓ You are an ambassador for Christ, show your light.
- ✓ You know with God anything is possible.
- ✓ You can make a difference with the help of God.
- ✓ You have the peace of God, that's beyond all understanding.
- ✓ You know God has much more in store for you.
- ✓ You realize that God has destined you for greatness in His Kingdom.
- ✓ You are to be a good example for all those you know.
- ✓ You are to be a person of integrity,
- ✓ You pray and encourage others often.
- ✓ You are a witness to others with your life.
- ✓ You show your love always.

HOPE IN GOD #1

Note: First read the 13th chapter of the Book of Daniel in the Old Testament of the Bible.

In this 13th chapter of Daniel is a story that tells of two evil men and a lady called Susanna. I won't tell you the whole story; you really do need to read it. One item of great interest is the aspect of hope.

Susanna had hope in her God. She was caught in a dilemma that seemed impossible; it seemed as if there was no way out. So Susanna cried out aloud, "O eternal God you know what is hidden and are aware of all things before they came to be…" Daniel 13:42

Within the context of this story, we see an unfailing dependence upon Almighty God. Susanna was faithful and felt that God was going to save her some way, somehow. In the end, justice was served and she, who was sentenced to death, was saved by Daniel. The last sentence in Chapter 13 was of primary interest "… God saves those that hope in him."

Question: Do you have hope in God?

HOPE IN GOD #2

I find in this world, in the flesh there are many problems, many misfortunes, day after day. My home with God in heaven, forever and ever. The days of this life are short, they consist of things in the world:

- There are wars and rumors of wars
- Life is full of sorrow
- There is evil in the world
- We have many unholy passions

- Many people are riddled with fear
- There are many distractions
- We are sinful at times
- We have erred in so many ways
- Many are broken and troubled
- We are weak and tempted

I want to strive to holiness. My spirit is stirred with thoughts of heavenly things. I desire to be with You Father; I pray this through your son Jesus Christ, with the Holy Spirit. This is my greatest desire:

- To be with the Trinity forever
- To call my home Heaven
- To accomplish heavenly things
- To be in a place with heaven and happiest
- To be in the presence of pure love
- To enjoy peace forever
- To receive your mercy and grace
- To receive your forgiveness for my sinfulness

I pray for all my impurities to be put away. I pray for things of goodness and love. I pray with all the angels in heaven for Your love and holiness

HOPE IN GOD'S LOVE

"… Hope does not disappoint, because the love of God has been poured out into our hearts through the Holy Spirit that has been given to us." Romans 5:5

Through the Holy Scriptures we find:

This Holy Spirit of God leads us and guides us. We learn about the love of God. We learn about the love of God.

We learn that the Father sent his only begotten Son. We learn that His Son Jesus Christ died on the cross to save us from our sinfulness. Jesus came to eliminate death and as a new Adam to bring us to new life. Jesus came to reconcile us to the Father. Wow!

Each of us wants eternal life in heaven. To live with the Father, Son, and Holy Spirit forever and ever. What a hope we have! I started off with a piece of scripture that says "hope does not disappoint." The love of God is poured out, into our hearts. With the Holy Spirit living within, who testifies to God the Father and the Son. We do have new life!

Jesus came to do the will of the Father. Jesus came down from heaven to bring about salvation to the world. The scripture points out:

"For this is the will of my Father, that everyone who sees the Son and believes in him may have eternal life, and I shall raise him (on) the last day." John 6:40

Below is a poem I want to share:

I LOVE YOU LORD GOD ALMIGHTY

> I will praise you, Lord, with all my heart
> I love you – Lord God almighty
>
> I will tell of all your wonderful deeds
> I love you – Lord God almighty
>
> I will sing with joy because of you
> I love you – Lord God almighty
>
> I will sing praise to you Almighty God
> I love you – Lord God almighty

CHAPTER 2

HOPE THAT GROWS

WHERE IS THE GOD?

As we move into Chapter 2: we find our hope is growing. Elijah was the Lords prophet. When his enemies killed all of the other prophets, he fled. Elijah was afraid for his life. He most likely wondered where God is.

He was visited by angels while he slept. The angels told him to eat and prepare for a journey. He ate and drank and prepared for the journey. Strengthened by the food, he walked forty days and forty nights, to the mountain of God.

On the mountain Elijah took shelter in a cave. The word of the Lord came to him, "Why are you here, Elijah?" He was told to go outside before the Lord God.

Where was God?

A strong wind came, but the Lord was not there.

After the wind there was an earthquake, but the Lord was not there.

After the earthquake there was a fire, but the Lord was not there.

After the fire was a whisper.

When Elijah heard this, he hid his face: a voice said to him, "Elijah, why are you here?"

Are you waiting to hear from the Lord God? Do you think something dramatic must happen to be a message from God? Are you waiting for a booming voice from heaven? Or do you think God, might just be in the whisper that we hear within?

Have faith and hope that God will lead you and guide you. We can hear him within our heart, with a tiny whisper, from the Holy Spirit within. Listen!

HOW HAS GOD REVEALED HIMSELF TO ME?

I was touched by the Spirit of God as a young child. When attending a church as a young age of maybe five or six years old; I went through a unique experience. I was asked a number of questions in a darken room. I was with an older lady in that room alone and to the best of my recollection I was asked the following questions:

Do you believe that Jesus is the Son of God?

Do you believe that he came down from Heaven?

Do you believe that he died on the cross for our sins?

I answered yes to all of these questions and then was asked:

Do you believe that he is our personal Savior?
Yes, was my response! This was a significant emotional event (SEE) for me. I accepted Jesus as my personal Savior

that day asking him to reside in my heart. Today I call that the Holy Spirit residing in my heart.

I also have encountered God (or he has revealed himself to me) in a number of other ways:

- ✓ Through other people
- ✓ Through a liturgical service
- ✓ From bible verses I have read
- ✓ Praying to God
- ✓ Meditating about God
- ✓ Through my studies about God
- ✓ Seeing God in nature
- ✓ Hearing the Holy Spirit talk to me
- ✓ Internally in the quietness of my heart

The above is just an overview of how God has revealed himself to me. There are probably dozens more if I meditated on the question further. I guess I could say: I know what I know! It is an experience I have within (my spirit) not something I can see outwardly.

GOD'S LOVE FOR US

The Bible gives us some insight into God's love for us. It tells us what God gives us, what he provides us, and his total love for us. The following comes from the Bible, the Old Testament, from the book of Isaiah (The following lines are found in Chapters 40, 41, 42, 43, 44, 45, 46, and 49 of Isaiah).

> You that hope in the Lord
> will renew your strength;
> You will soar on eagles' wings

You who are deaf, listen
You who are blind, look and see
Fear not, for I am with you

I have brushed away your offenses
The Lord, your redeemer
I carry out the plan

To those in darkness
Prisoners: come out!
They shall not hunger or thirst

I am the Lord and there is no other
I am God, there is no other
I will make you a light

THE PRESENCE OF GOD

My soul is touched by God
My life is sustained by God
My emotions are stirred by God
My spirit is encouraged by God
My physical body is graced by God
My prayers are answered by God
My faith, hope and love is from God

HOPE IN GOD'S WORD

Sometimes we think: How can I receive eternal glory with God? I wonder if I can become like the Father, Son, and Holy Spirit? Am I able to become united with them in spirit and love? Below is a guide on how to get there:

"Be merciful, just as your Father is merciful. Stop judging and you will not be judged. Stop condemning and you will not be condemned. Forgive and you will be forgiven." Luke 6:36-37

As we read the above comments from scripture, see that it is hard to implement into our lives. We understand as we read; but we wonder If It can be done? With the Holy Spirit dwelling within, leading and guiding us, it can be done. What is hard for us as ordinary human beings is easy for God.

So, we realize that we can become good, loving, and caring. We can help others, be nice, and understanding toward others. We strive to reach higher levels of love, agape love, love that is unconditional. Let us become closer to God, let us become like God in his attitude, and let us emulate Jesus Christ showing perfect love. Incorporate the following into your behavior:

>Be merciful to others
>Be forgiving to others
>Be nice to others
>
>Stop judging others
>Stop condemning others
>Stop hating others
>
>Be generous to others
>Be empathic to others
>Be light to others
>
>Understand others
>Care for others
>Love others

With the guidelines the scripture gives us, we know internally what must be done. We start to understand the nature of God and want his attributes to be incorporated within us. With the Holy Spirit nothing is impossible we can change the nature of man, with unity of the Trinity within. We can more God like; we can unite with the Trinity. After all we are made in the image and likeness of God. The nature of God is love, our nature can be love.

JUST SAY "YES"

We all know that Mary accepted the words of the Angel Gabriel. Then she said "yes" to become the holy vessel of our Lord Jesus. The Holy Spirit over shadowed her and she became pregnant. She gave birth to the Lord of Lords, the King of Kings, our Lord and Savior.

What about you? Do you say "yes" to small promptings from the Holy Spirit within your heart? Do you talk to someone you should forgive and reconcile a hurt when prompted? Are you prompted to say a prayer for someone and say "yes" to that prompting?

Below are ten items that will help us get closer to God. They will help us with getting to God's will, not so much as our will. Seek the Kingdom of God first. Let us all say "yes" to the following ten items:

TEN ITEMS THAT WE ALL SHOULD SAY "YES" TO:

1. Doing good whenever possible
2. Saying things of encouragement
3. Praying often when prompted
4. Try to see love in others
5. Giving of our time to help someone
6. Sharing what we have with others
7. Forgiving another to reconcile a hurt
8. Saying loving, caring words to others
9. Giving someone a hug when they need it
10. Trying to "Show Love Always"

As we mature in our walk we will gain more faith, hope, and love. We will exhibit the virtues that will show others God within. The grace that is given to us is passed forward with our actions.

TRUST IN THE LORD WITH ALL YOUR HEART

Trust in the Lord, have faith, do not despair (Ps27:14)
Trust in the Lord with all your heart

Relieve me of my worries and save me from all my troubles (Ps25:17)
Trust in the Lord with all your heart

The Lord protects me from all danger, I will never be afraid (Ps27:11)
Trust in the Lord with all your heart

The Lord is my shepherd, I shall not want (Ps23:1)
Trust in the Lord with all your heart

I will not be afraid, Lord, for you are with me (Ps23:4)
Trust in the Lord with all your heart

HOPE IN LIFE

Just how difficult is your life? Does your life seem to be full of tribulations? Does your life seem to be full of struggles? Does it seem to be one of toil and strife? Does it have one tragedy after another? Most will say, yes. But, that's just life; we can't expect everything to be great or fantastic all of the time. Life has its ups and downs. Sometimes life is hard and sometimes wonderful. We all have struggles and we all have times of great joy. Try to stay positive and upbeat.

What we need sometimes when things are difficult and we feel like giving up; to look forward to what awaits believers in Heaven. You need to have hope, keep believing that God will take care of you; give you what you need. We can't always receive what we want, but God will provide you what you need.

Life sometimes turns upside down. Some people will blame God. They expect that God will take away all of their hurt and pain. With prayers, asking for God's help: all prayers are answered and not all are received. Sometimes it seems as if God is waiting to fulfill our prayers, but we need time to accept what God has answered. God's ways are not our ways and we need time to process what His will is for us.

The answer to life's ups and downs is: attitude, the way we think. We need a positive attitude – expect everything will work out. We need to feel everything will be alright. Another aspect of a positive attitude is the way we think about God. Do you truly trust in the Lord? Do you feel that God answers prayers? This attitude will bring about hope in the darkness of life. We can feel the light of God's love and be transformed. We might even say during some struggle we have, to let this be God's will to pass this tribulation by me. We will be inspired with the grace of God, this will give us faith and realize God's divine will and desire for us, we will trust that will, and know God will provide divine assistance, because He loves me.

JOY TO THE WORLD

During Christmas, as you open your gifts last time, did they fill you with joy? Does the Christmas season fill you with joy? Are you filled with joy when you get together with your family? Hopefully, your response to these three questions is yes.

You know, it is in giving you feel joy more than when you receive. Where do you think this joy comes from? Is it the essence of life eternal from God? Is it supernatural or divine? It is the ecstasy of love, we give to others from God, and it channels through us. It is as giving a part of yourself to someone. If God lives in us from our baptism, when we become a child of God. Then this action alone could very well give us joy. We must nurture this joy and love of God, having faith and hope in Him that leads us home, we must stay true to His word and commands to continue in His love and Joy.

When the Christ child "Jesus" came into the world, joy came into the world. Then when Pentecost happened, more joy came into the world. When you get baptized more joy comes into your world, into your life. As you live a holy life of love toward God and toward one another, more joy comes into your life. The divine spirit of God, the Holy Spirit, within wants you to have joy. Embrace the joy that is there from God!

A PRAYER FOR JOY

Heavenly Father, give me more Joy. Let my heart be filled with your light and feel the warmth of your Holy Spirit. Let this warmth emanate to others. Let my joy give others your joy. Let this joy move others to love. Let this joy give others peace and patience. Let them show kindness, forgiveness, and compassion to others. In Jesus Christ's name I pray. Amen.

HOPE IN THE RESURRECTION

Most of the time when I think of hope I think of heaven. I think that with my faith and the hope in in the Lord Jesus I will receive eternal glory. The first believers had the same thoughts. With Jesus reconciling us with God the Father, with his death on the cross, we will have new life. We believe in the resurrection!

It has been said, "There is no Christian Religion without the resurrection of Jesus." This resurrection is what drove many of the original disciples to Jesus to continue the journey forward. During the persecution, the beating, and death of Jesus; many of his believers ran off and responded they didn't know him. They believed that the messiah would lead them to a new life. After the resurrection of Jesus, the disciples believed even more of Jesus' message.

The new law of love was acknowledged by many. The love of God sending his only begotten son and the love Christ had for us to die for our sins. As the Scripture says, in John 3:16, "For God so loved the world that he gave his only Son, so that everyone who believes in him might not perish but might have eternal life."

John the Baptist and Jesus' message was: to repent and change, to love God and their neighbor. This is the Good News to be with God forever and ever. This brings about the desire to be with God in heaven.

As the story goes about Paul's encounter with Jesus (See: Acts 26). "I appoint you, to open their eyes from darkness to light …"

OUR HOPE IN HEAVEN

If you have faith, hope, and love within your heart you have the three theological virtues within. Let us strive for the virtues that are available from God. These virtues are given as a gift from God himself. You must want to receive them, want them to lead you, and desire them with your heart.

In *The Word Among Us,* I found a sentence that is very significant toward the hope that is within us; "The very reason He (Jesus) became man was to testify to the reality of heaven and to make a way for everyone to join him there."

If you are asked: Do you want to go to Heaven? What is your answer? Most will say, yes! If we read in Revelation (Rev 21:1-4) the words about heaven we find that God will dwell among the human race. This will be a place of peace, joy, and happiness. We will be with our creator! Every tear will be wiped away, no more suffering, and no more death. There will be no more mourning. There will be no more pain.

What a place! An everlasting place of peace, tranquility, and joy. A place of pure holiness and love. This place is so wonderful, Jesus left it to come and tell us about it. Heaven is the home of all who believe Jesus is Lord.

Through the death and resurrection of Jesus, we are given the opportunity to have our sins wiped away. The divide between us and God is closed. Jesus' offering on the cross reconciled us with God. This reconciliation allows us to gain access to heaven through Jesus Christ.

In addition, on Pentecost, Jesus sent the Paraclete, the Comforter to help us on our journey. The Holy Spirit will lead us and guide us to the promise land, to heaven. This spirit allows us to have the love of almighty God in our hearts today. We strive to show love always to our families and friends. To let the light of Christ shine through!

HOPE IN JESUS #1

Jesus is our hope. We need to turn to Jesus for hope. He can heal us and help us overcome the difficulties in life. He can change circumstances. If you are sick He can heal us. If you are in a bad relationship He can help heal it. If you are lonely He can help eliminate loneliness. Jesus can help those rejected, divorced, and in despair. Pray and ask for His help.

Jesus can heal us. While walking the shores of Galilee, Jesus healed and spoke of God's love for us. His words are words of life, peace, and love. God, Jesus, the Holy Spirit, the Holy Trinity; is the same yesterday, today, and tomorrow. The supernatural power of God's healing can take place, in the here and now. We can be healed. I heard once that these healings', all miracles, point that God is real and are to fulfill God's will.

So, have hope in Jesus. His healing of us, whether for a physical infirmity, a relationship, or the mental anxiety you may want to resolve. Jesus has God's power to heal us. Jesus came to ask us to repent and reform our ways. To love God with all your soul, heart and mind and to love one another. Jesus asks us to believe in God and his supernatural power. Believe it and receive it. Have hope in his love and healing.

HOPE IN JESUS #2

In chapter 6 of the Book of John, Jesus gave a discourse entitled the "Bread of Life Discourse" to his disciples; Jesus talks about the "food that endures for eternal life." He first refers to the manna in the desert that God gave them. Then Jesus stated "I am the bread of life."

There was something at the end that was very important. He stated he came down from heaven to do the father's will. Then he went further to state what the Father's will is:

"For this is the will of my Father, that everyone who sees the Son and believes in him may have eternal life, and I shall raise him on the last day."

If you read the above statement closely, you will find he states everyone who sees the Son. Does that mean only the disciples that actually saw him? Does that mean the followers and Apostles who lived with him and saw him day in and day out? Or Does that me us also?

Remember the story when Jesus, after he had died, when he talked to, two of his disciples on the Road to Emmaus? In the scripture in the Book of Luke, Chapter 24, verses 13 to 35, it recounts what happen on a trip to Emmaus by two of Jesus' disciples. As they walked along with who they thought was a stranger to them, they talked about the scripture and the events of the day. Jesus had been crucified and died. Now the stranger, who was really Jesus, referred to the scriptures and interpreted them to the disciples.

In his interpretation of the scripture he pointed out; how from Moses to the prophets, they had referred to Jesus the Messiah who was to come. It was not until "he took bread, said the blessing, broke it, and gave it to them." Then their eyes were opened and they recognized him. Then they recounted how their hearts were burning when he opened the scriptures to them. But the final verse says it all: "Then the two recounted what had taken place on the way and how he was made known to them in the breaking of the bread."

We are the same! The Holy Spirit leads us and guides us with the scriptures and the words of Jesus. At times our hearts are on fire for the Lord Jesus. We gain knowledge and understanding from the scripture, as we hear them and they are interpreted for us. Finally, we gain the true wisdom of God in the breaking of the bread when we see Jesus? We see him in our hearts! We are coming to the point of doing God's will. We see the son and believe in him. Finally, in this belief we may have eternal life!

THERE'S HOPE IN THE CROSS

Within the book of Numbers, Chapter 21, there's a story about the Israelites complaining. The story goes on to say that God sent a punishment. The punishment was in which many people become ill and died from the bite of serpents. God wanted their trust, not their faithless complaining. Once the people saw their sin they repented. Moses prayed from them and God gave them a way to be healed. He told Moses to mount a bronze serpent on a pole. It anyone had been bitten they would look at the serpent and would recover, they would be healed. Note: This is the symbol our medical professionals wear today on their uniform.

They symbol that the people used to be healed physically is the forerunner to the crucifix. Today the crucifix is used to heal us spiritually. We look upon the cross, to remind us of Jesus' sacrifice and love for us. When our faith has transcended the doubt in our heart to trust, we are well on our way to be saved. Our trust in God is that he sent his only begotten son that we might live. With this hope that God gave us, through the sacrifice of Jesus, we can be saved.

THE HOPE OF THE PASSION

What does the word passion mean to you? Well if you look it up in the dictionary you probably will get something about emotion, but it also refers to the suffering that one might go through. Within the context of Jesus: the suffering of Jesus from the Last Supper to his death.

Jesus' passion has given us the opportunity to overcome death; we have been reconciled to God. We have the opportunity to accept Jesus as Lord and Savior. We have the opportunity to receive eternal life in Heaven with God forever and ever.

To help set the stage: if you study the scriptures carefully you will find prophesy or predictions about the passion. Jesus went to Jerusalem with his disciples and made predictions about what was coming about. He was fulfilling Zechariah's prophecy empathizing the King who comes.

We are pretty sure that the Jewish people waiting for the Messiah, was wanting not a king of gentleness, but a king who would over throw the Romans. They mostly expected that the Messiah would re-establish the Jewish people, the chosen ones, as a leader of nations. The believers in God expected a king on a stallion, a war horse, with legions of angles to take back what they considered was there's.

Most of the Jews did not understand about the humility and gentleness aspect of Jesus. His behavior was the true reflection of God, the Father, who sent him. The Jews wanted the Messiah, but though they would be put above all nations. They didn't really realize that Jesus was coming to die on a cross, to be an offering for all people, to reconcile us to God. He is the Lord, the Lamb of God, who takes away the sins of the world, to all who believes. It is our choice. What do you believe? As we look at the Passion of the Lord, we find parallels between Jesus and ourselves:

- ✓ He didn't want to die, neither do we!
- ✓ He cried with a sorrowful heart, so do we!
- ✓ He wanted to go to the Father, so do we!
- ✓ He knew humility was the way, so do we!
- ✓ He knew people were against him, so do we!
- ✓ He had a painful broken experience, so do we!
- ✓ He suffered from pain, so do we!
- ✓ He died in the end, so will we!
- ✓ He arose to everlasting life, ... (It is your choice)

One of the most, famous sayings in the Bible (paraphrased from memory below):

"God so loved the world, that he gave his only begotten son, that we might have eternal life."

Noticed the word *might* in the scripture. Why does it say *might*? Do we have to do certain things while here on earth? Are we being tested? Let's see if we follow the example of Jesus Christ:

- ✓ Jesus was baptized by John; are you?
- ✓ Jesus was test by the devil; are you?
- ✓ Jesus showed humility and obedience to God the Father; do you?
- ✓ Jesus followed the Ten Commandments; do you?
- ✓ Jesus knew there was a Hell; do you?
- ✓ Jesus knew there was a Heaven; do you
- ✓ Jesus knew we all run the race; do you?
- ✓ Jesus knew the answer was from God's mercy and grace; do you?
- ✓ Jesus showed us life is in love and service; do you?
- ✓ Jesus showed great love, by laying down his life!

So, do you accept the offering of Jesus for your sins? Do you humble yourself before God day after day? Do you accept Jesus as your Lord and Savior? Are you getting or have been baptized into the family of God; with water in the name of the Father, Son, and Holy Spirit. Do you strive to live a holy life with the Trinity? The answers to all the questions above are very important indeed. They may have the answer of the ages and might give you eternal life in Heaven for ever and ever. What hope we have in Jesus!

THE SUFFERING SERVANT

He is the great suffering servant
Praise God

He was beaten for our sins
Praise God

He startled many people
Praise God

He endured our sufferings
Praise God

He was pierced for our offences
Praise God

He took on himself our guilt
Praise God

He was the Lamb of God
Praise God

He gave his life as an offering
Praise God

He suffered for our justification
Praise God

He won pardon for our offenses
Praise God

Chapter 3

HOPE THAT MATURES

Our hope is now maturing. We have gone from some basics about hope and with that we continue with it to a higher level of maturity. We start to understand about God's love for us and the immensity of it all.

GOD'S LOVE

>Your love God is so big
>It is bigger than the biggest tree
>It is bigger than the biggest mountain
>
>Your love God is so large
>It is larger than the largest ocean
>It is larger than the whole world
>
>Your love God is so great
>It is greater than the greatest sunrise
>It is greater than the whole universe [11]

TRUE KNOWLEDGE

We have brains, which help us to learn and know about things. We know that knowledge is valuable and good. One item of importance is how is the knowledge used? Is it used for good, loving, and caring things? "All true knowledge, whether it is practical, theological, or philosophical, is meant to help us to love God and serve our neighbor, it's meant to help us share His good news and build His kingdom here on earth."

I have said many times that after knowledge, comes understanding, and after understanding comes wisdom. The scripture tells us, God will give you wisdom if you ask for it. Ask God for wisdom! Know the difference between knowledge, understanding, and wisdom! [12]

YOUR HEART

God has written love into your heart. He wants you to know His everlasting love. This love can overcome: fear, hate, rejection, suffering, discouragement, hurt, loss, and sin.

Remember God is there with His love to console you, to forgive you, to comfort you, to show you love, joy, and peace. He helps us and guides us with His everlasting light; the light of truth and love.

In Psalms 33 we are told that: God looks with love upon those who place all their hope in His love. Our Heavenly Father God Almighty, king of the universe gives us hope in His everlasting love.

And in Psalms 86 it says: "You are good and forgiving, full of love to all who call upon Your name." Therefore, let us call on the Lord God for His help and love. Ask God to give you the love that surpasses all understanding, that Agape love, the unconditional love from God Himself.

GENEROUSITY

Lord, teach me to be generous! Teach me to serve you! Teach me to give! Teach me to love you with all my heart and soul. Amen – Ignatius (Paraphrased)

HOPE IN UNITY WITH CHRIST

To obtain peace in our hearts about God the Father, Jesus, and the Holy Spirit; we must be in sync with them. We must obtain a place in our life where we feel we are doing good. We must feel our life is worth something; that we are to be to service to the greater good. We should consider more than ourselves, we are to consider our brothers and sisters, all of mankind. We are focused on things from above; we will be less likely to fall to the temptations of sin. We have a hope in unity with the Trinity.

The door to our heart, to our soul is our eyes, ears, and mind. Do we strive for the good? Do we strive to be better? Are we cultivating virtues within? We focusing on love? If we answer yes to the above questions, we may be well on our way to Christ like thinking. We must put our eyes, ears, and mind to good use.

The first step in a hope of hope toward becoming united to God is awareness. We must be aware we are from a fallen nature and we are sinful. All have fallen short of the glory of God. All have sinned. Within our thoughts we have a humble attitude toward God.

The second step in hope is to try to do something about our fallen nature. Remember with God anything is possible. We can overcome sin with virtuous thinking. Keep in your mind that the most import thing is not something temporal, but eternal. What is it you may ask? Your soul! You will last forever and that can very well be with God if you want. You must cooperate with the Holy Spirit. You must always try to do what is right and holy. Keep your words holy.

The third step of hope is to progress from thoughts, words, to deeds. We might think and talk Christ like; but only God can judge with what is inside of us. God knows what is in our heart. Are we truly in our soul, seeking first the Kingdom of God? Are we putting our thoughts and words into action? Our deeds will often show our actual intent, show what is from the inside, what is in our heart. We need to be a person of integrity! Do you walk your talk?

In conclusion, a journey of hop is one of thought, words, and deeds. It is a three-step process to become better, to overcome sin, and to take on the virtues of goodness and love. With the help from God; the Holy Spirit inside will lead us and guide us to unity with Christ. We will become more holy and find our way home to God (the Trinity) forever and ever.

HOPE FOR OTHERS

Once you have accepted Jesus Christ as your Lord and Savior, you feel holier. When you have been baptized you are a child of God, you feel holier. In other spiritual activities whether communion, confirmation, or an alter call, you feel holier.

Once you feel as if you are a child of God, maybe even forgiven and filled with grace. Once you feel that you are maybe even on your way to Heaven, it is hard to continue that within yourself. You feel, you need, to share it with others, especially family members and friends.

This feeling to share the, Good News is an internal desire to share God's holy love. We want to love and serve the Lord; we want to share the Good News. We want to move from self-centeredness to others centered. Listen to others and respond to their thoughts and listen to what the Holy Spirit is telling you to say. When reading scripture, ask the Holy Spirit what this means for them and you. Your faith will support you and have hope that your word will be given and received. The hope you have within, is shared to others.

FRIENDSHIP

> Friendship is like a Sunrise
> Beautiful and Warm
>
> Friendship is like Ocean Waves
> Constant and Enduring
>
> Friendship is like a Strong Tree
> Sheltering and Protecting
>
> Friendship is like a Mountain
> Expansive and Strong
>
> Friendship is like the Son
> Sharing and Caring

HOPE TO MOVE FROM SIN TO HOLINESS

Do you feel sinful, dirty, and awful? Are you guilty of your sinfulness? Do you have an anxiety that will not allow you to believe, sometimes, that God can forgive you? Our nature cries out for pleasure, passion, and even evilness at times. We think; "How can I be more holy?" The Bible is written to help us gain faith, hope, and love. When we read it, we see people with the same struggles, temptations, and sinful passions as we have. Take a look at a couple of examples:

Paul asked Jesus to remove the thorn from his side. He felt a spiritual conviction of something that caused him guilt. Just like us.

Thomas doubted Jesus had really been raised from the dead. He thought everyone was seeing things, they had an allusion; Jesus is not really alive. Until Jesus showed him the nail holes in his hands, he wouldn't believe. We doubt al times like Thomas.

Peter said he was ready to die with Jesus. When Jesus was arrested and had been being beaten, Peter denied Jesus on three occasions to save his own skin. He didn't want to be better and to die, like Jesus. Neither do we.

These three stories will give us hope that we are just like the great apostles. We fall short of the glory of God. We need our sins to be washed away by Jesus. We need to ask for forgiveness. We need to repent of our short comings. Our unfaithfulness is forgiven, we are children of the Almighty God, we are given grace to over some our short comings. We have moved from sin to holiness. We have hope!

PRAYING WITH HUMILITY

We are in a constant struggle while in this temporal order of our human nature. To obtain virtues that are heaven sent; strive for goodness and perfection that is of God. God will give us his divine love and send virtues of goodness to the degree in which we love him. God's special love is given to those who love and serve him, whose spirit is aligned with his own. He wants to help those who are conforming to his will. Almighty God will hear and answer those who are praying with humility of Jesus Christ.

HARMONY

The harmony of song is
Joy to the soul

The harmony of two people is
Peace for the two

The harmony of nature is
Light to the world

The harmony of love is
Music for the heart

LISTEN TO THE VOICE

A lady wakes up to take care of her baby. During the time with her child she remembers a dream she had. The dream was about two friends she knew from college twenty years ago; it was a dream of concern about their father. She emailed the concern to one of them who was a Priest now; who forwarded the email to his father.

The email is received by his dad right after one of the sons told him in a phone message "Mom wants you to do this test. You ought to do it, just as a preventive measure. It's not risky. And it would make her feel good."

The father with no other symptoms had been losing energy. Not feeling sick just, a little weak, which he took it as getting older. After an annual exam and a treadmill test with a Cardiologist; he told him to take another test. But he was reluctant and the doctor told him he could wait for six months if he wanted to. So, he decided not to take the test.

You can see where this is leading, right? The forwarded email was received directly after the phone message his son left for him. Bob Morris decided to get the test done. The doctor said something like this after the test, "It's a good thing you took the test. The heart had a 90% blockage, if you would have tried to wait for the six months you would have had a massive heart attack."

Remember there were no symptoms! Let us all listen to the voice within. [13]

HOLY ANGER

The Bible says Be angry but do not sin; do not let the sun set on your anger, and do not leave room for the devil. It seems like a condition. If it is blended with ill will, it becomes sinful.

If we become gantry we sometimes are unleashing, fury, hate, and hostility. When this is unleashed it changes very quickly into sin. If we are going to follow Christ, we are to be kind, humble, patient, and merciful. We are to forgive and love. So, we need to keep a leash on our anger. We need to keep anger under control at all times and be humble and patient.

I had a friend ask me, how do we do that? With guidance from the Holy Spirit, using humility and patience up front, if any ill will is felt, turn away immediately and ask the Holy Spirit to remove it from your heart and mind, but leave immediately. We don't unleash the anger and let the fury, hate, and hostility we have within manifest itself into chaos. God created calm from chaos! Let God, the Holy Spirit, give you Christ's peace, patience, and tranquility.

What is impossible for us, is possible for the Holy Spirit!

What is the Holy Anger? I thought all anger is sin? Isn't all anger sin? No! Did Jesus get angry and overturn the money tables? Did Jesus drive out the money changers? Yes! He was angry about something happening in God's house that was wrong. We may have anger, it arms the passions quickly against evil, and operates with the force and effectiveness of an instinct. The problem from there is don't allow malice to enter your heart. Provide an understanding, caring, loving mind set. Be patient, kind, and gentle in your approach. One word comes to mind besides mercy – thoughtful. Think it out, before acting.

Chapter 4

HOPE THAT TRANSFORMS

Hope that is transformed from the ancient wisdom is good for us. It is found within the Holy Scriptures and is indeed very valuable to us. But we all realize that there is a true wisdom, something more profound. Realize that wisdom is from God!

ANCIENT WISDOM

Ancient wisdom can be
Found in ancient writings

Ancient wisdom can be
Found in the Scriptures

Ancient wisdom can be
Found in the writing of Solomon

Ancient wisdom is not true wisdom
True wisdom is found in God

PAUL'S HOPE FOR US

When the Apostle Paul wrote the letter to the Philippians he had a hope for unity and humility. That same hope is passed on to all Christians. If I asked you who the Bible is written for? What is your answer? It should be – ME! The Bible is written for each one of us. The Holy Scripture is written to change us. It is God's Holy Word. This word from God through the inspiration of the Holy Spirit is God's story; which will give each of us our faith, hope, and love.

So even though the letter to Philippians was written for the people at that time, it also relates directly to us. In the second chapter it starts with a hope or a plea for unity and humility. Paul refers to the encouragement in Christ. We all need encouragement. He goes on to reference love, compassion, mercy, joy, and of course love again. When we show compassion, mercy, and joy; we show love from our heart. Love is all encompassing!

When Paul refers to love, he is presenting a point of view that is one of humility. Becoming of the same mind and united in heart. Can you imagine! Paul states that we need to do nothing out of selfishness, but humbly regarding others as more important. This is agape love. The unconditional love from God! We all need to strive toward unconditional love. We all need to reflect the love of Christ.

Therefore, we all need to strive toward a Christ-like attitude. An attitude of humbleness toward, not only God; but a humble attitude toward all people, toward one another. Christ did this and more! He took it another step forward. Christ not only came down from heaven, but he was obedient to the Father. He died on the cross for – US!

At the end Jesus died on a cross reconciling us to God. He humbled himself so much, to the obedience of death on a cross. He followed through with God's great plan to bring us into his family. We become children of God through Christ's blood on the cross.

So, what is your response to this? We all personally must accept Christ as our savior. This is an individual decision to internalize scripture pertaining to Christ and then to confess that Jesus Christ is Lord. What then? Paul goes on to say in the next six verses to work out your salvation. God wants us all to work toward his glory. We need to use our gifts and talents to glorify God. We are to be "like lights in the world." We are to provide sacrificial service!

OBEDIENCE AND SERVICE IN THE WORLD

Jesus came to do the will of the Father. Jesus came down from heaven to bring about salvation to the world. The scripture points out in John 6:40 "For this is the will of my Father, that everyone who sees the Son and believes in him may have eternal life, and I shall raise him (on) the last day."

MOVING FORWARD

May all your future endeavors be fruitful.
May you have good times in abundance.
May you embrace those times of joy.
May you rise to the occasion when needed.
May you challenge yourself to love greatly.
Remember, Love is above
all accomplishments
that one can obtain from any endeavor.

WITNESSING FOR CHRIST

<u>The Lord Calls us</u>: to become part of his family. We need Jesus and the Holy Spirit to reach God the Father. Our commitment is: To love God with all our heart. To love God with all our soul. To love God with our mind. To love God with all our will. Always remember to seek first the Kingdom of God.

<u>Further Growth</u>: is done through bible study, renew type programs, small faith groups, life in the spirit type seminars, conferences, prayer groups, and religious education classes.

The Lamb of God "Jesus" asks us, and invitation, to experience a fuller life and to be united with the Spirit of God. Jesus reveals the Father and his love, by giving his life for us, accepting the Fathers will. The supreme example of love – Jesus giving his life for us. He is the vine we are the branches.

<u>Our Response to the Lord</u>: to as that our sins are forgiven. Our sins are equated as our refusal to love God fully, to do his will. We are rejecting his love through our sin. Sin keeps us from being what we are meant to be.

The mission of Jesus is to set us free, to redeem us, to reconcile us to God, to heal us, and to make us whole again. The Lords asks us to act justly, to love, to walk humbly in obedience with God.

<u>Discipleship</u>: to follow Jesus is to commit ourselves to do good and to encourage one another. To show Love for one another, to imitate Jesus. To say "I live no longer, but Christ lives in me." To love God will all our heart, mind, soul, spirit, will, and strength.

WITNESSING FOR CHRIST … MORE

Each Christian has his or her own way of developing their spirituality. Each of us studies the scriptures, read a daily devotion, read a spiritual book, go to a conference, attend a retreat at a monastery, or something to help in our own spiritual development. We should include others and tell others about the Good News. As I was reading in my daily devotional, I found a short piece about witnessing. I thought this is important, because Jesus wants us to share this Good News to others. We are part of the great commission.

No matter the career or the work we do, one job we have is, to help in building the Kingdom of God. We all should be using our talents and resources to build the Kingdom. Life is a journey toward a higher level of love "Agape Love" to a higher level of spirituality, holiness, which lead us to communion with God.

No matter what your job is – your job is also helping to build the Kingdom. We all should be led by the Holy Spirit, to show love, appreciation, and joy. We need to exhibit kindness, forgiveness, and compassion in our everyday actions. We need to think about things from above. In our thoughts, words, and deeds we need to exhibit the gifts of the spirit. Think about it! We need to let our light show to others in this dark world. Our life should conform to Christ – we can come to the point that we say – "I no longer exist, but Christ within exists."

You need to work for God – glorify God!

OUR LOVE HAS GROWN

In our beginning years
Love has been sown

Throughout the years
Our hearts have grown

In our final years
Our love has grown

Chapter 5

THE JOURNEY CONTINUES

HOLY SPIRT
LEADING YOU AND GUIDING YOU

God the Father, Jesus the Son, and the Holy Spirt are all one; the Trinity. Therefore, when I say God it is all of them who work in concert together. Their everlasting love is for you. Their mercy and grace are for you. They are encouraging you guiding you.

- ✓ God says "Do not be afraid."
- ✓ You are a child of God.
- ✓ You are one of God's holy children.
- ✓ God has a plan and you are part of it.
- ✓ God has a role for you to play in his plan.
- ✓ You are a member of God's family.
- ✓ You need to show other's kindness.
- ✓ God has called you to show love.
- ✓ God wants to give you everlasting joy.
- ✓ You are to be his light.

- ✓ You are to show others forgiveness.
- ✓ God wants you to be an instrument of Peace.
- ✓ God wants a personal relationship with you.
- ✓ You are to tell others about Jesus.
- ✓ You are to share the Good News.
- ✓ God wants you to read the Bible.
- ✓ God wants you to listen to his holy word.
- ✓ You are to exhibit peace in your actions.
- ✓ You are to be patient with others.
- ✓ God wants to provide you with what you need.
- ✓ God will supply you with your needs.
- ✓ You need to show compassion to others.
- ✓ You are to have a generous heart.
- ✓ God wants you to pray to him daily.
- ✓ Go wants you to depended upon him.
- ✓ You need to worship God daily.
- ✓ You need to love God with all your heart.
- ✓ God wants to encourage you to greatness.
- ✓ God wants you to be holy.
- ✓ You need to transform your spirit.
- ✓ You need to be born again.
- ✓ God will lead you down a path or righteousness.
- ✓ God will guide you to holy actions.
- ✓ You need to listen to the Holy Spirit within.
- ✓ You need to follow the Holy Spirit's guidance.
- ✓ God wants you to be faithful.
- ✓ God wants you to serve Him.
- ✓ You need to surrender your pride.
- ✓ You need to become humble.
- ✓ God has sent his only begotten son for us.
- ✓ God has been reconciled to us through Jesus.
- ✓ You have been cleansed from all your sins.
- ✓ You have salvation and through Christ.
- ✓ God knows your heart.

- ✓ God wants you to be holy and loving.
- ✓ You can transform your life.
- ✓ You can become holy and loving.
- ✓ God can fill you with his divine light.
- ✓ God can give you extraordinary love.
- ✓ You can grow and prosper in love.
- ✓ You can become a person of great love.

As you read through the above information you have changed. You can develop into a person of greatness with love and appreciation toward others. You can be infused faith, hope, and love. You can be led by the spirit. You are transformed into a deep spirituality, a deep conversion, a deep holiness, toward the Father, Son and Holy Spirit. You can have peace and joy in your heart.

PRAISE GOD AT ALL TIMES

Give thanks to the Lord, our God
Praise God at all times

Sing to God a new song
Praise God at all times

The Lord's word is true and trustworthy
Praise God at all times

Go, King of the Universe, made the heavens
Praise God at all times

The Lord spoke and it came to be
Praise God at all times

God's plan is salvation for all who believe
Praise God at all times

The Lord fashions our hearts and minds
Praise God at all times

God's eyes are upon the reverent
Praise God at all times

The God show us kindness and forgiveness
Praise God at all times

God loves us and all of creation
Praise God at all times

PRAISE GOD FOR HIS GRACE

Praise God for His Grace
You bless those who obey you Lord,
Your love protects them like a shield
(Psalms 5:12)
Praise God for His Grace

The Lord hears my cry for help
He listens and will answer my Prayer
(Psalms 6:9)
Praises God for His Grace

God is my Protector
He saves those who obey him
(Psalms 7:10)
Praise God for His Grace

The Lord is a refuge for the oppressed,
A place of safety in times of trouble
(Psalms 9:9)
Praise God for His Grace

The Lord is righteous and loves good deed
Those who do them will live in his presence
(Psalms 11:7)
Praise God for His Grace

THE STEPS TO HOLINESS

LET ME ADDRESS SOMETHING THAT'S VERY IMPORTANT:

Remember that God so loved the world that he sent his only begotten Son that we might have eternal life. Also, that Jesus Christ loved us so much that he offered Himself up for us, for our sins. Believe that the Holy Spirit was sent to us to help us to love God and to help us to love our neighbor. The key word is to BELIEVE.

LET US BOW OUR HEADS IN PRAYER:

In the name of the Father, the Son, and the Holy Spirit.

- Let us all make a choice to follow Jesus, to understand if we see Him, we see the Father.
- Let us all make a choice to become a child of God to love Him with all our heart.
- Let us all make a choice to worship God with full devotion, obedience, and love.
- Let us all reflect the character of Jesus Christ, showing love always with Kindness, Forgiveness, and Compassion.
- Let us all become Ambassadors for Christ.

OUR FATHER

Our Father who art in heaven, hallowed be thy name. Thy kingdom come; Thy will be done on earth, as it is in heaven. Give us this day our daily bread, and forgive us our trespasses, as we forgive those who trespass against us, and lead us not into temptation, but deliver us from evil. Amen

PRAYING THE PSALMS

> Happy are those who trust in the
> Lord and can say, here I am Lord.

Over the years I have been to a number of retreats. In one of these retreats I was asked to make a presentation. Our focus for this particular weekend retreat was on the Psalms. I choose to pray all 150 Psalms. I choose to find the essence of each of the Psalms in a short sentence or phrase.

The application of this is below: It was or course entitled, "Praying the Psalms," I would read each one and then the group, with the same handout, would repeat what I had just read. This is like a responsorial. In this matter we actually prayed all 150 Psalms. It was quite an experience for all. Note: be prepared to take some time – it takes a while!

1. The law of the Lord is their joy.
2. Happy are those who take refuge in God.
3. You Lord, are my shield.
4. I Trust in the Lord.
5. To you I pray, O Lord.
6. Have pity on me, Lord, for I am weak.
7. You are the God who saves.
8. Our Lord, how awesome is your name.

9. I will praise you, Lord, with all my heart.
10. The Lord is king forever.
11. The Lord is just and loves just deeds.
12. Lord, protect us always.
13. O God, Give light to my eyes.
14. The Lord restores.
15. Never be shaken.
16. You will show me the path to life.
17. Lord, listen to my prayer.
18. I love you, Lord.
19. The heavens declare the glory of God.
20. May God send help.
21. There's joy in your presence.
22. I will proclaim your name.
23. The Lord is my shepherd.
24. Seek the face of God.
25. I lift up my soul.
26. In the Lord I trust.
27. The Lord is my light and my salvation.
28. The Lord is my strength and my shield.
29. Bow down before the Lord.
30. Lord, be my helper.
31. Let me never be put to shame.
32. I confess my faults to the Lord.
33. By the Lord's word the heavens were made.
34. I will bless the Lord at all times.
35. I am your salvation.
36. How precious is your love, O God!
37. Trust in the Lord and do good.
38. Forsake me not, O Lord.
39. You are my only hope.
40. To do your will is my delight.
41. Lord have mercy on me.
42. My soul longs for you, O God.

43. God, defend me.
44. You are my King and my God.
45. Nations shall praise you forever.
46. God is our refuge and our strength.
47. The Lord, the Most High, inspires.
48. Great is the Lord.
49. God will redeem my life.
50. Offer praise by your sacrifice.
51. Have mercy on me, God.
52. I will praise you always.
53. All have gone astray.
54. O God, hear my prayer.
55. The Lord will save me.
56. In you I trust, I do not fear.
57. I call to God Most High.
58. The just shall rejoice.
59. Rescue me from my enemies.
60. With the help of God.
61. Hear my cry, O God.
62. My soul rests in God alone.
63. O God, I long for you.
64. I take refuge in the Lord.
65. May we be filled with goodness.
66. Shout joyfully to God.
67. May God's face shine upon us.
68. God is our salvation.
69. I pray to you, Lord,
70. Graciously rescue me, God.
71. You are my rock, my hope.
72. May his name be blessed forever.
73. Lord God you are my refuge.
74. You God, are my king.
75. We thank you, God.
76. You are an awesome God.

77. Your way, O God, is holy.
78. Trust in God.
79. Pardon our sins.
80. God save us and restore us.
81. Sing joyfully to God.
82. Rescue the lowly and poor.
83. Lord, the Most High.
84. Happy are those who find refuge in the Lord.
85. O Lord, I will listen to your word.
86. Teach me, Lord, your way.
87. Within you is my true home.
88. I cry out to you, Lord.
89. Love is established forever.
90. May we gain wisdom of heart.
91. My God in whom I trust.
92. I proclaim your love.
93. Holiness belongs to your house, Lord.
94. Happy are those you guide
95. Hear his voice.
96. Sing to the Lord.
97. The Lord is King.
98. Shout with joy.
99. Exalt the Lord, our God.
100. Love endures forever.
101. I act with integrity.
102. Lord, hear my prayer.
103. Bless the Lord, my soul.
104. The Lord endures forever.
105. Give thanks to the Lord.
106. Happy are those who do right.
107. God is our Savior.
108. Awaken my soul.
109. Save me in your kindness.
110. I begotten you, says the Lord.

111. I praise the Lord with all my heart.
112. Our hearts are tranquil, without fear.
113. Praise, the servants of the Lord.
114. The God of Jacob.
115. Our God in heaven.
116. I love the Lord.
117. The Lord is faithful forever.
118. Give thanks to the Lord.
119. Walk by the teachings of the Lord.
120. Lord, deliver me.
121. The Lord is my guardian.
122. May those who love you prosper!
123. To you I raise my eyes.
124. Our help is in the name of the Lord.
125. Trust in the Lord.
126. The Lord has done great things.
127. The Lord builds the house.
128. Walk in the ways of God.
129. The blessings of the Lord be upon us.
130. With the Lord is kindness.
131. I have hope in the Lord.
132. Let us worship God.
133. The Lord has life for evermore.
134. Come, bless the Lord.
135. Praise the Lord; the Lord is good!
136. God's love endures forever.
137. We sit mourning and weeping.
138. You strengthened my spirit, Lord.
139. Lord, you know me, you understand me.
140. Deliver me, Lord, from the wicked.
141. Lord, I call on you.
142. You are my refuge.
143. Lord, hear my prayer.
144. My shield, in whom I trust.

145. My God and king.
146. The Lord protects.
147. Sing to the Lord with thanksgiving.
148. Praise the Lord's name.
149. Let the faithful rejoices.
150. Give praise to the Lord!

CHAPTER 6

THE FINAL STEPS

Now we have come to a point that I call the final steps. We need to continue our spiritual development, our spiritual journey in hope that not only matures, but transforms us. A maturity that truly transcends us into the dimension of spirituality. Since we started, we have within us more faith, hope, and love. Throughout, the book I have included some of my poems, mediations, and prayers. I will continue that within this chapter – I have been asked by a number of people to share them.

LONGING FOR GOD

As the deer longs for running streams
So my soul longs for you O'God

My very being thirsts for you O'God
When can I see your face?

I wait for your O God
I praise you my Savior, my God

At the dawn may the Lord bestow love on me
I sign praises night and day to you O'God

You are my rock and salvation O'God
I praise you my Savior my God

Reference is Psalm [42]

GLORY TO YOU O'GOD

I will bless the Lord at all times
Glory to you O'God

My soul will glory in the Lord
Glory to you O'God
Magnify the Lord at all times
Glory to you O'God
Let us exalt His name together
Glory to you O'God
Lord deliver me from all my fear
Glory to you O'God
I sought the Lord and He answered
Glory to you O'God
Look to God that you may have joy
Glory to you O'God
The Lord heard me and saved me
Glory to you O'God [18]

GOD OF THE UNIVERSE

Sing to the Lord of Heaven and Earth
Sing to the Lord a joyful song

Announce his salvation has come
Announce his mercy and grace has come

Give honor, glory, and praise to the Lord
Give worship to the Lord your God

His kindness endures forever and ever
His mercy and grace is never ending

Give thanks to the Lord, for he is good
Give thanks to the Lord, for he is kind

Praise the Lord your God with all your heart
Praise the Lord his love is beyond all understanding [19]

SACRIFICE

The Lord God,
Gathers his faithful together

The Lord God,
Does not want animal sacrifices

The Lord God,
Wants praises as your sacrifice

The Lord God,
Wants you to call on him during distress

The Lord God,
Will rescue you from your distress

The Lord God,
Wants you to honor him

The Lord God,
Wants you to be obedient

The Lord God,
Will show you salvation [20]

JESUS IS THE LORD

The Lord Jesus Christ is the redeemer;
You were known before you knew him

The Lord was there at the beginning
You were there later

The Lord is the shepherd;
You are a part of his flock

The Lord leads you in the path of righteousness
You will walk in the valley of death

The Lord will give you goodness and kindness
You will fear no evil

The Lord will give you love and forgiveness
You will follow the Lord all your days

The Lord will give you mercy and grace
You will dwell in the Lord's house forever [21]

AL MOZINGO

A SONG OF LOVE

O Heavenly Father I love you
Jesus and the Holy Spirit

I give you my heart and love
Give me your heart and love

I pray to you day and night
Please listen to my prayers

I repent and ask for forgiveness
Forgive me of all my sinfulness

I thank you for sending me your Son
Let his grace dwell within me

I want to become closer to you O'God
Send the Holy Spirit to lead me

I thank you for Jesus my Lord and Savior
Please let me dwell with you forever and ever

Amen

I LOVE GOD

I love God with all my heart

I love God with all my soul

I love God with all my spirit

I love God with all my mind

I love God with all my strength

I love God with all my will

I love God with my whole being

TRUE WISDOM

Your trust is from God
Trust in the Lord

Your strength is from God
Trust in the Lord

Your heart is from God
Trust in the Lord

Your hope is from God
Trust in the Lord

Your testing is from God
Trust in the Lord

Your deeds are from God
Trust in the Lord

Your reward is from God
Trust in the Lord

Jeremiah 17:5-11

THE WAY

Josemaria Escriva the founder of Opus Dei in 1928 wrote a book entitled *Spiritual Considerations;* this book was later called *The Way*. Much of what Josemaria wrote about is how an ordinary person can live a life for God. I used it as a guide to write a brief, compact, summary. This summary in many ways is written in contemporary terms; so, the information was rewritten, reformatted, and restructured.

The vision of my book is to have people increase hope and to raise their prayers to God by the use of this small book. To help them in their faith, hope, and love. To help guide them to the heavenly light from above. To guide them to God the Father, Jesus Christ the Son, and the Holy Sprit the comforter. To lead them toward showing love always. Remember that Jesus Christ is the Way, the Truth, and the Life! Jesus Christ is the Lord!

In my first book: *Extraordinary Love* I carried this information from the numbers of 1 to 68. In my second book, *Extraordinary Faith* I carried from 70 to 170. In this book *Extraordinary Hope*, I have listed 171 to 271.

- Always show love! (171)
- Be a prayerful soul. (172)
- Keep everything that leads you to God. (189)
- Cast out everything that leads you away from God. (189)
- Conquer yourself each day with God's help. (191)
- Work for the salvation of other souls. (192)
- Show tolerance and understanding toward others. (198)
- Conquer your pride with God's help. (200)
- Humble yourself! (201)
- Show generosity toward others. (202)

- Atonement leads to life. (210)
- Purify yourself with humility. (212)
- The pure light of love will not fail you. (212)
- Tears can purify your past. (216)
- Give up this life for eternal life. (218)
- Be generous, Jesus will fill you with grace. (221)
- Penance will help you to obtain eternal life. (224)
- Your worst enemy is you. (225)
- Treat your body with charity. (226)
- Fasting is pleasing to God. (231)
- Examination of your conscience should be done daily. (235)
- Examine yourself with courage. (237)
- Always ask for the light to fill you. (240)
- Strive to acquire all good virtues. (241)
- Your debts are paid with tears and with works. (242)
- Examine yourself: Why have you gone astray? (243)
- Listen to the Holy Spirit. (244)
- Your resolutions should always be specific. (247)
- Make few resolutions; fulfill them with God's help. (249)
- Always give God the glory, the honor, and praise. (252)
- Strive to conduct yourself well today and tomorrow. (253)
- Work for Christ. (255)
- Know that your pain will turn to joy and peace. (256)
- God can give you peace; it surpasses all understanding. (258)
- Obey the loving and sacred heart of Jesus Christ. (259)

- Strive for joy in your heart; reject sadness. (260)
- God has given us back our soul though Jesus Christ. (261)
- Forget the sins from the past; they have been forgiven. (262)
- Today's struggle is training for victory. (263)
- Fill yourself with faith, hope, and love. (264)
- Realize that you are always in the presence of God. (256)
- Consider all decisions with God's help. (266)
- Remember God is always near to us. (267)
- God is love; helping us, inspiring us, and blessing us. (267)
- God is a loving Father, who will forgive us always. (267)
- Make a habit of giving thanks to God. (268)
- Jesus is our model of love; today, tomorrow, forever. (271)

Note: The number at the end of each saying reflects a number that corresponds with one of the 999 points that is put forth in *The Way* by Josemaria Escriva, Image Book, Published by Doubleday, Random House, Inc., New York, New York.

LOVE IS A POWERFUL FORCE

Love is the most powerful force in you
Love can change sadness to happiness
Love can change anger to understanding
Love is the most powerful force in the world
Love can make the impossible possible
Love can make peace where there is conflict

> Love is the most powerful force in the universe
> Love can change darkness to light
> Love can change hate to love

The following has been put together to share with you in order to improve your prayer life. This information came from a retreat that the Pastor of our church presented to the staff members. I am providing to you an overview of this information.

BENEDICTINE PRAYER
LECTIO DIVINA

To enhance our prayer life I have added the Benedictine Prayer formula. Lectio Divina is a method of prayer that extends back to the fourth and fifth centuries. It is translated as "scared readings" using the Bible as the base of the prayer, using four steps: Reading, Meditation, Prayer, and Contemplation.

<u>Lectio</u> (Reading) – uses the word of God (or other spiritual readings). Writings in the Bible have been inspired by the Holy Spirit; understand that God inspires others also. Some say works of art can also be used.

<u>Meditatio</u> (Meditation) – uses meditation (thinking/intellect) to reflect on insights. Personalize the message with how does it pertain to me? Bring to life the meaning of the Word to your daily life.

<u>Oratio</u> (Prayer) – uses one's feelings to enter a dialog with God with prayer. Your response to an insight obtained and what changes you want to make in your life. Next, incorporate the Word of God into your heart and into your very life.

Contemplatio (Contemplation) – uses one's intuition to coalesce the experiences of the first three steps by contemplating the insights obtained. This is a time just to be quiet, to listen to the Holy Spirit within. This fourth step is also referred to as "Resting in the Lord" it is Contemplative Prayer.

We can be assured that our Lectio Divina has been successful and God has truly touched us when: we have an increase of the virtues. Through the Word of God in Galatians 5:22-23 we can summarize these virtues we want in our life as: [22]

Love	Joy
Peace	Patience
Generosity	Faithfulness
Kindness	Gentleness
Self-control	Purity

AUGUSTINIAN PRAYER

The Will of God

To enhance our prayer life I have added the Augustinian Prayer formula. The Augustinian Method of Prayer has been used by the Fathers of the Church throughout hundreds and hundreds of years. The key word to help describe this Augustinian Prayer is transposition. Through this transposition process one uses his or her creative imagination with the words of the Scripture. To lead us to our situation today. One tries to imagine the words of the scripture spoken to him or her today.

Throughout the course of history several writers, preachers, teachers, and ordinary lay people have used this method. This process is aligned with intuition and feeling of the participant. The person using this method has an interest in the current application and with future possibilities. The participant tries to discern the will of God within today's context.

Through the Bible God speaks to us. Through prayer we speak to God. When using this method, we develop a dialog between God and our self. With meditation we strive toward a personal development of our relationship with God. One personalizes the insights obtained through this process to discern God's will. Being able to penetrate the wisdom of God, bring it down to earth, applying it to our own situation, and determining the will of God is the hope of many. One needs to be open to the Holy Spirit's promptings to discover the deeper meanings within the word of God.

This dialog between God and oneself can be accomplished by using the four steps of Lectio Divina: Reading, Meditation, Prayer, and Contemplation.

Ask the following questions: What this Scripture mean to me? – And – What is the Lord trying to say to me? [23]

IGNATIAN PRAYER

Spiritual Exercises

About a thousand years before the birth of Christ the Israelites prayed in a way that commemorated its history, salvation history, recalling specific events. The Israelites celebrate their Passover Event yearly, commemorating their deliverance from the slavery of Egypt.

Christians have continued the use of this type of prayer; specifically, Saint Ignatius of Loyola, the founder of the Jesuit Orders used this under the title of Spiritual Exercises. When using this type of prayer, the participant projects themselves into the historical happening, becoming a part of the event. The best example of this type of prayer by Christians today is Holy Week.; beginning in Palm Sunday through Easter Sunday. It commemorates each part of the Passion, Death, and Resurrection of Jesus Christ.

Out of a since of duty the Participant uses Scripture stores to draw their mind and heart into the past. In addition, new insights allow one to advance in their spiritual growth on their journey toward God. This type of prayer allows one to draw practical insights and then progress in their life of faith. The purpose is to try to make the Scripture Scene become alive and real to the participant. It allows one to commemorate and to internalize the message.

Using the four-step process of the Lectio Divina is common to the use of this type of prayer: Reading, Meditation, Prayer, and Contemplation.

Saint Ignatius also developed a ten-step process to be used during his Spiritual Exercises. [24]

1. Choose the Topic
2. Prepare the Prayer
3. Put yourself into the Scene
4. Pray for Grace
5. Reflect on what you see
6. Reflect on what you hear
7. Reflect the whole process
8. Try to draw practical Insights
9. Unite with the Trinity
10. Closing with a prayer of the "Our Father"

FRANCISCAN PRAYER

The Love of God

Saint Francis of Assisi, from the thirteenth century, has an attitude of openness and willingness to follow the Spirit. This type of prayer is marked by a spirit of being free, unconfined, and allowing the Spirit to move him or her. The person who prays a Franciscan type prayer is committed to do God's will and is not tied down by rules.

The person inclined to pray in this realm is cheerful, light-hearted, optimistic, and they thrive on challenge. Franciscan spirituality is for all of us. We should be committed to acts of loving service; fraternal love in doing God's will.

Franciscan spirituality is optimistic, seeing the beauty of God's creation. In addition, they are led by free-flowing, spontaneous, informal praising, and loving dialog with God. In addition, they are very forgiving in their attitude. It is said that Franciscan Prayer makes use of all of our senses.

One important aspect is that Francis Assisi understood that the Incarnation of God, Jesus, the actual presence of God; who came down from Heaven.

Another aspect of Franciscan Spirituality is their motto "Seize the Day" which follows the teaching of Jesus: Do not be concerned about tomorrow. It will have troubles enough of its own. Sufficient for the day is the trouble thereof. (Matthew 6:34)

Franciscan Spirituality is interested in the literal since of the Bible; they are interested in reality of the Scripture to their lives. Many of the greatest saints, who showed an enormous amount of generosity prayed with this method. They love spontaneous prayer to celebrate the goodness, greatness, and love of God. [25]

THOMISTIC PRAYER

Praying with Rational Thought

This particular method of praying is associated with the name of Saint Thomas Aquinas, because it uses a method of rational thinking. It is also known as a Scholastic Method of praying in orderly, progression of thought. Close attention is the process of rational thinking to arrive at appropriate conclusions.

Most Christians from the seventeenth century to the twentieth century have been using this method. It certainly is used by many who have written about meditation and a rationalistic approach to prayer. To use this method of prayer in the preparation for the Sacrament of Reconciliation is an excellent choice.

This is adaptable to men and women who thirst for the truth, knowledge, understanding, and trying to comprehend the word of God. In addition, the person who prays this form of pray would have a tendency to perfectionism, are impatient with incompetence, and will criticize others because of their own high standards. They may be unduly demanding, very competitive, and are fascinated by power. They are similar to the modern-day scientist, investigating the causes behind the word or others actions. They are very systematical in their approach to the Word of God.

This type of pray is logical, rational, and meditation. The Thomistic prayer seeks the truth. One way of accomplishing this is to ask the questions of: who, what, where, when, and why.

The method used to pray with this is Lectio Divina. This dialog between God and oneself can be accomplished by using the four steps of Lectio Divina: Reading, Meditation, Prayer, and Contemplation. [26]

RETREATS

Now I am presenting from my journal notes on retreats that I have attended and retreats that I have presented. Within the context of those pages I will pass on the lessons learned and the spiritual insights from my notes. I believe this information will help provide lessons on love, faith, and hope.

To grow in our spiritual life, we need to advance ourselves spiritually. Jesus said to learn from me: you will find peace in your heart through these lessons. Be humble in your actions; serve God and others. This is part of our path to heaven, by putting these lessons into use, and into action. Always chose what is good and pleasing to the Lord; this is the will of God. Give God glory and honor; seek first the Kingdom to God.

A RETREAT

Retreat experiences are opportunities for participant to withdraw from the stresses and distractions of daily life. A retreat is:

- A time Spiritual enlightenment
- A time of solitude
- A time for Reflection and meditation
- A time for prayer
- A time to discern your spiritual call
- A time to respond to God's call

SPIRITUAL FACULTIES

The Cloud of Unknowing

To help with your development as a Christian or Contemplative you should know the basics. Information and knowledge are the first steps in transformation of your heart. In the book *The Cloud of Unknowing* written about 500 years ago by an unknown author helps us gain that information and knowledge. The author indicates that by our nature we are gifted with three primary and two secondary faculties.

<u>Three Primary Spiritual Faculties</u>
1. Mind
2. Reason
3. Will

<u>Two Secondary Spiritual Faculties</u>
1. Imagination
2. Feeling

Working with all of your faculties – one can transcend themselves – with the grace of God.

<u>The Mind</u>:
The mind is the principal power to comprehend spiritual realities with the help of reason, will, imagination, and feelings. All these other faculties will help and support the mind in its understanding. Therefore, the mind's task is to work with the others or understand. The mind helps on to receive, then sort through thoughts, and then retain knowledge. In addition, the mind can embrace and control the will.

Reason:
 Reason allows us to distinguish from what is bad and from what is good. Reason also allows us to determine what is better or best. Reason is blinded as a consequence of Original Sin, unless it is illuminated by grace of God.

Will:
 The will helps us to move toward the good. The will also takes into account our love and desire. It finally rests in the will with a feeling of satisfaction. We reason with our mind and we determine what is good, then we cause our self (our will) to move that direction.

Imagination:
 Our imagination will allow us to visualize things that are absent. We can see things in the present, past, or future. Imagination never ceases day or night give us a view or to distort the image of things because of Original Sin. Imagination can allow us to visualize spiritual things within our minds. If this is done without the grace of God it may be wrong. Therefore, it can actually present a false reality in your mind.

Feeling:
 Our feeling is the faculties of our soul which extends to the senses and helps us interpret the world around us. It helps us to experience exterior and interior senses. Feelings help us understand internally pleasure and pain. (Mad, Sad, Glad) Without grace, Feelings would give itself up to the pleasures of life and of the flesh. Therefore, man would degrade into a beast instead of a human being with a spiritual destiny. One last thought, in *The Cloud of Unknowing* it states that feelings are the servant of the Will. Most of us believe it to be the other way around.

Note: We have talked a lot about Original Sin; all faculties were sound (we can actually say we were of sound mind) before Original Sin. Originally man was in no danger of choosing and loving a false good because of his or her primordial integrity. With his or her faculties sound we were not liable to be deceive by them.

However, man fell and disobeyed God. Understand that man cannot consistently choose the good without God's grace. Original Sin left man wounded and blind so that he is easily deceived; understand that an evil can disguised itself as good.

As you grow in self-knowledge and human perfection, your spiritual faculties will develop into good habits. If we are grace by God our bad habits are conquered and we form good habits. This is a transformation closer to union with God and love. [28]

THE PRESENCE OF GOD

> My soul is touched by God
> My life is sustained by God
> My emotions are stirred by God
> My spirit is encouraged by God
> My physical body is graced by God
> My prayers are answered by God
> My faith, hope and love is from God

THE WORLD AS WE SEE IT

Do you believe the world is really as you perceive it to be? Is the world a place of hatred and discontent or is the world a place of love and understanding or is it a combination? We all put our own slant on the world because of our own learning, experiences, and personal disposition. We have changed the world internally. If this is true: Can we change the world externally?

It the world seems to you as a place of hatred with selfish people who are mean and nasty: What can you do? Do you respond back with the same kinds of behavior or do you take another path? It is your choice! Don't let someone else's behavior change your behavior. We are all faced daily with injustice and behaviors that will make us angry. We might even be affected emotionally or let's say we surely are affected emotionally. Do you let emotions take over? You can respond in kind or you can take another path. It's your choice.

If you want to see a loving world of generous people you might be disappointed. Because this is not what is going to happen, at least continuously. But, remember you have a choice of how you are going to respond. Every day there are numerous assaults occurring on you that you feel are unjustified. These assaults will provoke a response; many times, the response will not be a rational calm one, but an emotional outburst. You feel that you have been insulted, abused, or hurt in some way. This attack on you is usually followed with an attack back by you. I have a one-word suggestion – stop. Don't attack back, evil begets evil.

If we want to see a loving, caring, understanding, world of generous people we will have to be part of it. Our emotions have to be kept under control. Don't respond back with a vindictive response. Respond back with a calm loving, caring, understanding approach that helps someone else who is hurting and angry. Help your brother or sister in their emotional need with love. We can change the world!

SEEKING THE LIGHT

As a small flame becomes an inferno, so does a small light of God's love within become a beacon. The light of Christ within can show God's love to the world. We have been chosen to do good works. We have been chosen to let the light within shine. The light of God is there within; let it shine forth.

As we walk this earth, we seek something. We try to fill this void within, through people or things, but the feeling of emptiness is not fulfilled. It is because what we seek is not external, but within. Fulfilling that emptiness is done by God, his gift to us—the Holy Spirit. The Holy Spirit, God's gift, can give us happiness, peace, and joy.

Many people weep and are sad because they cannot find what they seek. They are in a circle of despair. The circle is a never-ending circle of sadness, depression, misery, fear, anger, conflict, helplessness, and despair. This circle can be broken or, let's say, transformed, into a circle of happiness. Remember, what we seek is not found in the external world. Remember, what we seek is not found in people or things. What we seek is a personal relationship with God. Most of us feel an emptiness, a longing for something, that emptiness and longing can only be filled by our Almighty God. The only thing that can fill the emptiness within — God.

We seek the light. This is the truth; this is God's message to us. That true happiness is within us. The acceptance of the gift of life, eternal life, and the light is what is needed. Jesus said, "Knock and the door will be opened; seek and you will find." Jesus said, "I am the way, the truth, and the life." If you want to replace the circle of despair with the circle of happiness, seek God.

With the grace of the Lord Jesus Christ, with the love of God, and with the fellowship of the Holy Spirit; we can find true happiness. Our inner feeling of emptiness can be filled with God's Spirit. We can replace the emptiness with love, peace, kindness, forgiveness, compassion, joy, patience, and happiness. Our inner joy can be a beacon to the world. True happiness can be found in the joy of Christ. Our love of God can shine on others through us. We can help others in their seeking by helping them realize that God's gift is there to be accepted. This helping is done through loving one another.

PRAYERS

Over the years I have used the Names of God The Father, The Son, and The Holy Spirit as a prayer to the Trinity. They are listed below:

PRAYING THE NAMES OF JESUS

    Jesus is the Author of Salvation
    Jesus is the Bread of Life
    Jesus is the Cornerstone
    Jesus is the Rock
    Jesus is the Alpha and Omega
    Jesus is the First and Last
    Jesus is the Root of David
    Jesus is the Messiah
    Jesus is the Anointed one
    Jesus is the Deliverer
    Jesus is the High Priest
    Jesus is the Faithful and True Witness
    Jesus is the King of Kings
    Jesus is the Lord of Lords
    Jesus is the Redeemer
    Jesus is the Gate
    Jesus is the Mighty God

Jesus is the Wonderful Counselor
Jesus is the Good Shepherd
Jesus is the Holy One
Jesus is Immanuel
Jesus is the Lamb of God
Jesus is the Light of the World
Jesus is the Mediator
Jesus is the Physician
Jesus is the Prince of Peace
Jesus is the Radiance of Your glory
Jesus is the Word
Jesus is the Savior of the world
Jesus is the Way, the Truth, and the Life

THY WILL BE DONE! (SAINT FRANCIS DE SALES)

These are basic concepts and ideas, the main points put forth by Saint Francis de Sales in fifty-eight letters written to help people in their adversities. As a bishop and spiritual director of countless souls, St. Francis actually wrote hundreds, maybe even thousands, to help people with problems of anger, frustration, grief, sickness, difficulties in prayer, lack of faith, and more. His work has been published continually since 1665, when he was canonized. He left us with a lasting legacy in his work, which called us to live a devout life in Jesus Christ and the ultimate call to holiness in the living God. The information below can be used to help one to meditate on God's will for one's life. These small sayings can also be used as a daily meditation.

The first is my interpretation of the response letter's focus or the essence of the response and then the comment in the book follows my comments from St. Francis de Sales.

1. Resign yourself into the hands of God. "Thy will be done"
2. Conform to the divine will of God. "Do the will of God joyfully"
3. Be faithful and morally right. "Serve God where you are"
4. Keep your heart on peace. "Let us be what we are and let us be it well"
5. Acquiesce to the Word of God. "Our faith should be naked and simple"
6. Pray to God and listen to God. "There are two principal reasons for prayer"
7. Commit yourself to charity toward others. "Little virtues prepare for contemplation of God"
8. Keep yourself in the presence of God. "We must remain in the presence of God"
9. Strive for simplicity of life. "Never does God leave us save to hold us better"
10. May Jesus live in your heart. "Marriage is an exercise in mortification"
11. Be a force of harmony in the family. "As far as possible, make your devotion attractive"
12. Exercise a gentle heart toward everyone. "Have patience with everyone, including yourself"
13. Maintain a spiritual calm about yourself. "Keep yourself gentle amid household troubles"
14. Rest your soul in God's love. "Do what you see can be done with love"
15. Strive to have patience in your life. "Parents can demand more than God Himself"
16. Be joyful and do good. "Avoid making your devotion troublesome"
17. Strive for tranquility of heart. "Have contempt for contempt"

18. Live in God's light and grace. "Lord, what would you have me do?"
19. Be polite and generous to others. "Take Jesus as your patron"
20. Fortify your spirit with spiritual exercises. "Remain innocent among the hissings of serpents"
21. Let us not judge another. "Never speak evil of your neighbor"
22. Unite yourself to God's holy love. "Extravagant recreations may be blameworthy"
23. Ask God for an abundance of wisdom. "We must not ask of ourselves what we don't have"
24. Resign your will to God's will. "If you get tired knelling, sit down"
25. Live entirely in God's will. "You will not lack mortifications"
26. Walk faithfully in the way of our Lord. "We must always walk faithfully"
27. Be a devoted servant to God. "Illness can make you agreeable to God"
28. Offer your heart to God. "You are being crowned with His crown of thorns"
29. Have patience in adversities. "Often the world calls evil what is good"
30. Have true humility of heart. "Rest in the arms of Providence"
31. Love and serve God in your vocation. "In confidence, lift up your heart to our Redeemer"
32. Take time each day to think about God. "We must slowly withdraw from the world"
33. Ask for God's help when you need it. "This dear child was more God's than your"
34. Thank God for his love and patience. "Think of no other place than Paradise or Purgatory"

35. Ask for God's will to be done. "How tenderly I love her"
36. May you suffer a loss with peace in your heart. "Calm your mind, lift up your heart"
37. Humble yourself to God's divine mercy. "Miserable beggars receive the greatest mercy"
38. Forgiveness of another will show your love. "Love God crucified, even amid darkness"
39. Occupy your heart with God's wishes. "Do not desire mortifications"
40. May your heart be ever united to God's. "Practice the mortifications that are given to you"
41. God give us peace in our troubles. "O good Cross, so loved by my Savior!"
42. Keep yourself gentile, humble, and patient. "You only want to bear the crosses that you choose"
43. Aspire to the pure love of God. "We must be patient as we seek perfection"
44. Have courage and a good heart. "Have courage, for you have only just begun"
45. Examine your heart when needed. "Be gentle and charitable to your soul"
46. Walk toward God with humility. "God loves greater infirmity with greater tenderness"
47. Be diligent in progressing of your spiritual life. "We must bear ourselves until God bears us to Heaven"
48. Show true charity to your neighbor. "Self-love can be mortified, but never dies"
49. Holy indifference to your life is a good approach. "We must attain holy indifference"
50. Ask God for his light to fill your spirit. "Lean on the mercy of God"
51. To change the world, we must change ourselves. "To change the world, we must change ourselves"

52. May we give witness to God's love. "In patience shall you possess your soul"
53. Ask God to help you during temptations. "Do not worry yourself about temptations"
54. Thank God for his grace and love. "We must not be fearful of fear"
55. Keep a purity of intentions. "Constrain yourself only to serving God well"
56. May Jesus live and reign in your heart. "True simplicity is always good and agreeable to God"
57. We must do everything with love. "We must do all by love and nothing by force"
58. Seek God with all your heart. "Be then all for God"

An approach to this life should be contentment. Maintain your faith, hope, and love. Exhibit kindness, forgiveness, and compassion — *KFC*.

A GRATEFUL HEART

I praise your holy name Lord
I exalt you over all others Lord
I thank you Lord with all my heart
Lord you strengthen my spirit
Lord I love to hear your holy word
Lord how great is your glory
The Lord cares for the lowly
The Lord saves me and loves me
The Lord is with me forever and ever [29]

LOVE IS A POWERFUL FORCE

Love is the most powerful force in you
Love can change sadness to happiness
Love can change anger to understanding

Love is the most powerful force in the world
Love can make the impossible possible
Love can make peace where there is conflict

Love is the most powerful force in the universe
Love can change darkness to light
Love can change hate to love

CLOSING PRAYER

O Heavily Father,
Thank you for your love.
Thank you for your Son Jesus Christ.
Thank you for sending us the Holy Spirit.
Thank you for the blessings that you have bestowed upon us.
We pray that the Holy Spirit will remind us of the lessons learned today.
We pray that the Holy Spirit lead's us and guide's us into your eternal love.
We pray that we are an example of your love and light into the world.
We pray that we are guided by the Holy Spirit to be good Christians.
In Jesus Christ's name we pray.
Amen

END NOTES

1. My Imitation of Christ, Thomas a. Kempis, Confraternity of the Precious Blood, 1982
2. Psalms 85, New American Bible
3. The Word Among Us, March/April, 2014
4. The Word Among Us, November 2014
5. My Imitation of Christ, Thomas a. Kempis, Confraternity of the Precious Blood, Book III, Chapter 28, 1982
6. 1 Kings 19
7. The Word Among Us. June 2, 2014
8. The Word Among Us, Dec. 24, 2014.
9. The Word Among Us, Feb/Mar 2013, St. Augustine, FL
10. John 6 and Luke 24, New American Bible
11. Isaiah 52 & 53, New American Bible
12. The Word Among Us, March/April, 2014
13. The Word Among Us, December 2014
18. Psalm 34:2-7
19. Psalm 96
20. Psalm 50
21. Isaiah 44 and Psalms 23
22. *Prayer and Temperament*, Different Prayer Forms for Different Personality Types; Chester P. Michael, Marie C. Norrisey
23. *Prayer and Temperament*, Different Prayer Forms for Different Personality Types; Chester P. Michael, Marie C. Norrisey

24. *Prayer and Temperament*, Different Prayer Forms for Different Personality Types; Chester P. Michael, Marie C. Norrisey
25. *Prayer and Temperament*, Different Prayer Forms for Different Personality Types; Chester P. Michael, Marie C. Norrisey
26. *Prayer and Temperament*, Different Prayer Forms for Different Personality Types; Chester P. Michael, Marie C. Norrisey
27. *Prayer and Temperament*, Different Prayer Forms for Different Personality Types; Chester P. Michael, Marie C. Norrisey
28. *The Cloud of Unknowing*, Image Book, New York, N.Y., 1973
29. Psalm 138

www.ingramcontent.com/pod-product-compliance
Ingram Content Group UK Ltd.
Pitfield, Milton Keynes, MK11 3LW, UK
UKHW022216230426
12048UKWH00016BA/878